Englisch lernen mit

Benjamin Blümchen™

für Kinder im Vor- und Grundschulalter

von Rosa-Maria Wagner

Max Hueber Verlag

Dieses Werk folgt der seit dem 1. August 1998 gültigen Rechtschreibreform. Ausnahmen bilden Texte, bei denen künstlerische, philologische oder lizenzrechtliche Gründe einer Änderung entgegenstehen.

3. 2. 1. | Die letzten Ziffern
2006 05 04 03 02 | bezeichnen Zahl und Jahr des Druckes.
Alle Drucke dieser Auflage können, da unverändert,
nebeneinander benutzt werden.
1. Auflage

Illustrationen: Friederike Spengler, Gablingen
Druck und Bindung: J. P. Himmer GmbH & Co. KG, Augsburg
Printed in Germany
ISBN 3-19-019491-2

Liebe Eltern,

ich freue mich, dass Sie sich für den Hörspiel-Kurs *Englisch lernen mit Benjamin Blümchen* entschieden haben! Sie halten das Bilderbuch zu unserem Hörspiel in den Händen, das liebevoll illustriert und gestaltet in 16 Szenen das Benjamin-Blümchen-Abenteuer darstellt und es damit in der Fantasie der kleinen Zuhörer noch lebendiger macht.

In unserer Geschichte werden Benjamin Blümchen und seine Freunde Otto und Karla Kolumna nach London eingeladen, um im dortigen Zoo mit Kindern und Tieren ein Jubiläum zu feiern. Auf der Reise und im Zoo erleben die drei viele lustige und interessante Abenteuer. Dabei macht Benjamin Blümchen auf seine liebenswerte Art und Weise die ersten Schritte in der englischen Sprache – und mit ihm die jungen Zuhörerinnen und Zuhörer.

Die unserem Kurs zugrunde liegende Methode ist exakt auf den kindlichen Spracherwerb zugeschnitten. In den ersten Lebensjahren haben Kinder die bemerkenswerte Gabe, sich eine Fremdsprache auf dieselbe spielerische Art und Weise anzueignen wie die Muttersprache, nämlich durch ein natürliches Eintauchen in die Sprache (Immersion), durch Hören und Nachahmen. Erwachsenen geht diese Gabe fast vollständig verloren. Daher ist das Erlernen einer Fremdsprache in späteren Jahren viel schwieriger. Kinder haben es da wesentlich leichter.

Unser Hörspiel bietet die Gelegenheit, viel Englisch zu hören, in einfach strukturierten Sätzen, die aus der kindlichen Erlebniswelt kommen. Da Hörgeschichten erfahrungsgemäß immer und immer wieder angehört werden, bekommen die Kinder auf diese Weise ‚Englisch ins Ohr'. Die Verbindung zwischen dem Gehörten und den Bildern führt dazu, dass Ihr Kind die Geschichte versteht – zunächst intuitiv. Nach mehrmaligem Anhören werden die englischen Wörter und Ausdrücke dann Schritt für Schritt genauso selbstverständlich wie die deutschen.

Schauen Sie gemeinsam mit Ihrem Kind das Bilderbuch an und lesen Sie, wenn Sie möchten, auch mal selbst einige der wichtigsten englischen Wörter und Sätze aus den Szenen vor, die in Sprechblasen und in einer Textspalte auf den Doppelseiten abgedruckt sind. Die deutschen Bedeutungen finden Sie im Anhang.

Meine Erfahrungen mit Englischkursen für Kinder in Kindergärten und in privaten Kursen haben mir immer wieder gezeigt, wie unkompliziert Kinder mit der Aneignung einer fremden Sprache umgehen und durch die Kombination von Hören und Sehen (= Erleben) Englisch viel schneller lernen, als wir Erwachsene uns das vorstellen können.

Kinder brauchen darüber hinaus die ermunternde Aufmerksamkeit ihrer Eltern oder Bezugspersonen. Schauen Sie sich daher das Bilderbuch gemeinsam an, so oft Ihr Kind Spaß daran hat, und erleben Sie, wie *Englisch lernen mit Benjamin Blümchen* zu einem Lern- und Spielspaß für die ganze Familie wird.

Viel Spaß und Törööö!

Ihre
Rosa-Maria Wagner

Ein Brief aus England

"Dear Mr Blümchen,
Please, come to our zoo in London. We need you for a celebration.
Otto is welcome, too.
These are your tickets.

Best regards, Mr Liontail,
Director, London Zoo."

Let's go to England together!

Wow, that's great, Benjamin!
English is easy and fun.
Yes, of course.

Good morning, everybody!
Hello Mr Blümchen!
Hello Mr Tierlieb!
Hi Otto!
My name is Karla Kolumna.
I'm Mrs Kolumna.

How wonderful!
Let's go to England together!
Tschüss, I mean – Goodbye!
See you tomorrow!

Richtig, Otto, du kannst ja schon Englisch sprechen. Dann will ich das auch lernen.
Yes, English is easy and fun.
Good morning, everybody! My name is Karla Kolumna. I'm Mrs Kolumna. Let's go to England together!

Let's pack the suitcase!

Benjamin, let's pack the suitcase.
This is a suitcase.
What do we need?
I need some trousers
and a jacket.
Right, a T-shirt, too.
Then I need my shoes.
Then my comb,
my toothbrush and toothpaste.

Now let's pack your things.
You need your pink pyjamas
and your pink night cap.
Then put in a packet of
sugar lumps.
What else do you need?
Right, your towel.
Put in your nice, fluffy towel.
And don't forget the soap.
Put in your alarm clock.
You never know.
Well done, Benjamin.
We've finished.
Yes, English is easy and fun.

Have a nice trip!

At last, Mr Blümchen, at last!
We're late! We'll miss the train!
The train is coming! Hurry up!
Yes, Mr Tierlieb, we've got
our luggage.
Yes, we've got our tickets
and our passports, too.
We've got everything, Mr Tierlieb.
Have a nice trip and have
a nice time.
Thank you, Mr Tierlieb.
Have a nice time, too.
All aboard!
Let's get in quickly!
Goodbye, bye-bye!

Goodbye!
Have a nice trip and have a nice time.
We've got our luggage.

Travelling

We've made it.

Train
Here comes the train,
here comes the train,
running along again.

Plane
Here comes the plane,
here comes the plane,
flying along again.

Car
Here comes the car,
here comes the car,
going so fast and so far.

Truck
Here comes the truck,
here comes the truck. –
Trucks, trucks all in a row,
trucks, trucks ready to go.

Bus
Buses, buses, all in a row,
buses, buses ready to go.

Great, Mr Blümchen, really great!

On the ferryboat

It's a really big boat
with an enormous anchor.
There are lifeboats.
Over there is the captain.
There are the sailors.
Let's get on board!
I hope I won't get seasick.
Listen, that's the horn.
We're ready to go.

Ladies and gentlemen,
welcome on board the "Old Mary".
Captain Nelson and his crew wish you
a pleasant journey to Dover.

Off we go!
Look at the captain, he's steering the boat.
Look at the seagulls, they're flying in the sky.
Look at the fish, they're swimming in the water.
Goodness! I hope there are no sharks or whales.
There are seals, but no dolphins.
Otto, listen – to the waves – and to the wind.
Marvellous!

Where is Mr Blümchen?
Oh look, Mrs Kolumna, there is Benjamin!
He's steering the boat!
How wonderful! Benjamin the captain!
I have to take a picture!

Welcome to London Zoo!

Hello, everybody.
I'm Mr Liontail,
director of the London Zoo.
Welcome to our zoo.
Thank you, Mr Liontail.
I'm Benjamin Blümchen from
Neustadt in Germany.
Nice to meet you, Mr Blümchen.
Are these your friends?
Yes, these are my friends.
This is Otto.
And this is Mrs Kolumna.
Mrs Karla Kolumna, a reporter
from the Neustädter Zeitung.
Nice to meet you, Mr Liontail.
Hello, Mrs Kolumna. Hello, Otto.

Look, these are my children.
Hello, my name is Jenny.
Hello, my name is Jack.
Hello, Jenny, hello, Jack.
Let's have a cup of tea.

I'm Benjamin Blümchen from Neustadt in Germany.
LONDON ZOO
Welcome to our zoo. These are my children.
TICKET
Hello, my name is Jenny.
Hello, my name is Jack.

Benjamin's home in London

Look, Benjamin, this is your house.
Do you like it?
Yes, I like it. It's beautiful.
Open the door.
Be careful, Benjamin.
Is the door big enough?
Yes, Otto, the door is big enough.
Don't worry.

Benjamin, this is your bed.
It's extra big.
Here is a table and some chairs.
There is a lamp and
here is a bunch of flowers.
Thank you, Jenny. I love flowers.
We also put a new green rug
on the floor.
And here is a fire-place and
there is an armchair.
Oh look, Otto, a fire-place!

I think it's time to go to bed now.
You must be very tired.
Good night, Mr Blümchen.
Sleep well, Otto.
Good night, sleep tight
and have sweet dreams.
Good night, everybody.

Good morning, Benjamin, the sun is shining!

Good morning, Benjamin!
It's time to get up.
The sky is blue
and the sun is shining.
And it's nice and warm, Benjamin.

Look, the weather is wonderful today.
It's not cloudy and not raining.
It's not windy.
And it's neither cold nor snowing.
Yes, it's a beautiful,
sunny day today.

Come on, sleepyhead,
get up and get ready.

Getting ready

Benjamin is waking up.
Benjamin is yawning.
Good morning, everybody.
Good morning, Benjamin.
Benjamin is getting out of his bed
and stretching himself.
Now Benjamin is in the bathroom.
He's singing.
He's taking off his pyjamas
and his night cap.
He's having a shower.

Now he's drying himself.
Oh, my nice, fluffy favourite towel.
Benjamin is getting dressed.
Otto, where is my red jacket?
Here it is, Benjamin.
And where are my
blue trousers, Otto?
Here they are – on the chair.
And here is your cap, Benjamin.
Thank you, everybody. –
I'm ready now.

Benjamin's body

It's your trunk.
Yes, a trunk is an elephant's nose.
It's quite a long nose.
But very useful.
And these are your ears, Benjamin.
Your ears are very large.
So, I've got a long nose
and two large ears.
Right. And two eyes.
And this is your mouth.
All this is your head.
But you haven't got any hair.
No, elephants don't have any hair.
Then you've got two arms
and two legs and two feet, too.
They are round and big
like your hands.
And you've got a tail. I like your tail.
Your tummy is the biggest.
It's round and fat – and empty.
Listen, it's rumbling.
I'm very hungry.
And I'm hungry and thirsty.
All right, let's have breakfast then.

I'm very hungry.
It's your trunk.
Your tummy is the biggest. It's round and fat – and empty. It's rumbling.

Let's have breakfast!

We've got tea and milk,
and toast and butter.
Here is the jam and the honey.
Do you like scrambled eggs, Benjamin?
No, I don't, sorry.
But I do. I love them. Mmh, yummy!
Here are some cornflakes.
And here are some delicious strawberries.
Mmh, strawberries!

Benjamin, what would you like to eat?
Oh, I'd like some strawberries, please.
Thank you. I love strawberries! Mmh!
Me too. They are so sweet.
And what would you like to drink,
Benjamin?
I'd like a cup of tea with ...
... lots of sugar lumps.
We know, Benjamin!

And what would you like to drink?
I'd like some strawberries and a cup of tea.
TEA
Cornflakes

Lots of animals

Come on, let's walk round our zoo.
Look, there are the pink flamingoes.
They're standing in the pond.
There are the bears.
And here are the lions.
They've got babies.
They are called lion cubs.
Oh, they're so cute.
There we've got the giraffes.
They're very tall with their long necks.
And over there are the elephants.

Here are the birds: owls and eagles and
... I'm Polly. I'm Polly.
And this is Polly, a talking parrot.

Hello, Polly. How are you today?
I'm fine, thanks. I'm fine, thanks.
Polly, I'm Benjamin Blümchen.
I'm Benjamin Blümchen.
No, Polly, you are not Benjamin
Blümchen. You're Polly.
You're crazy. You're crazy.

Hippo, snake, kangaroo,
camel, panda, peacock.

The *10* monkeys

I like the monkeys best.
They are so funny.
Look, this one is climbing up the tree.
And that one is hanging on a branch.
There are lots of monkeys.

How many monkeys can you see?
One, two, three in the tree.
Four are sitting on the floor.
One is at the door.
One is jumping like a frog.
And one is dancing on the log.

That makes one, two, three, four, five,
six, seven, eight, nine, ten.
There are ten monkeys. Good, Benjamin!

Balloons, colours and more

Stop, Benjamin, stop blowing!
It'll burst! Stop!
Bang! It's burst. What a pity!
That was a nice purple balloon.
Never mind. Here is another one.
We've got plenty of balloons.
Yes, balloons in all colours, look:
red, blue, green, yellow, pink,
purple, orange, and white.
There aren't any black, brown
or grey balloons. No, but here
are some colourful Chinese lanterns.
And we've got plenty of paper chains.

Hello, everybody. How are you?
What are you doing?
Oh, I see, you're getting ready
for the celebration. Can I help you?
Yes, Mrs Kolumna, you can.
All right, but first I have
to take a picture of you.
Please, keep smiling! Cheese!
Sensational! That's a great picture.

Here are some colourful Chinese lanterns.
Stop, Benjamin! Stop blowing! It'll burst!

The celebration

Englisch lernen mit Benjamin Blümchen

Lern-Hörspiel

Buch: Rosa-Maria Wagner

Regie: Ulli Herzog

Ton: Carsten T. Brüse

Redaktion: Hans Hillreiner, Max Hueber Verlag GmbH, Ismaning

Produktion: Jutta Buschenhagen, KIDDINX Studios GmbH, Berlin

Titelmelodie: Heiko Rüsse, KIDDINX Studios GmbH, Berlin

Die Rollen und ihre Sprecher:

Benjamin Blümchen:	J. Kluckert
Otto:	K. Primel
Karla Kolumna:	G. Fritsch
Herr Tierlieb:	E. Vaessen
Jenny:	J. Engler
Jack:	J. Reddig
Mr Liontail:	H. Cooper
Polly:	D. Reidies
Erzähler:	G. Schoß

Eine Produktion der KIDDINX Studios GmbH
Im Vertrieb des Max Hueber Verlages GmbH

Englisch lernen mit Benjamin Blümchen™

für Kinder im Vor- und Grundschulalter

von Rosa-Maria Wagner
illustriert von Friederike Spengler

Englisch lernen mit Benjamin Blümchen ist ein Sprachkurs für Kinder ab 3 Jahren.

Benjamin Blümchen und seine Freunde Otto und Karla Kolumna werden nach London eingeladen, um im dortigen Zoo mit Kindern und Tieren ein Jubiläum zu feiern. Auf der Reise und im Zoo erleben die drei viele lustige und interessante Abenteuer. Dabei macht Benjamin Blümchen auf seine liebenswerte Art und Weise die ersten Schritte in der englischen Sprache - und mit ihm die jungen Zuhörerinnen und Zuhörer.

Viel Spaß und **Törööö !**

Das Package besteht aus

- einer Sprachlern-Hörspiel-CD (40 min) mit den Originalsprechern der beliebten Benjamin Blümchen Geschichten,
- einem bunten Bilderbuch mit Illustrationen zur Hörgeschichte und Zusatz-informationen (Text in Sprechblasen, Ausdrücke und Vokabular, ca. 600 Wörter und Wendungen),
- und einem Vorwort mit Kurzanleitung für die Eltern.

Die Autorin **Rosa-Maria Wagner**
ist seit vielen Jahren als Lehrerin für Frühenglisch tätig und eine erfahrene Autorin und Trainerin im Bereich Englisch für Kindergarten- und Grundschulkinder.

9 783191 094911

www.hueber.de

Hueber

ISBN 3-19-109491-1

Look at all these people.
Even the mayor is here.
And a brass band!
Oh, I love brass band music!
Look, they've got lots of instruments:
trumpets, drums, saxophones ...
How exciting!
I can play the trumpet, too.
Great, Jack.
We've even got a choir.
They will sing some songs.
It really will be a wonderful celebration.
I must get my camera ready.
Sensational! I'm so happy.
And I'm happy to see all the children –
all the boys and girls.
They all want to see you, Benjamin.

I'm so nervous.
You'll manage it, Benjamin. I'm sure.

Ladies and gentlemen.
I welcome you to the
London Zoo's *150*th jubilee.
This year we have a very special guest:
Mr Benjamin Blümchen,
the talking elephant from Germany.
Let's listen to Mr Blümchen.

Benjamin's speech

Good luck, Benjamin.
Thank you, Otto.

Ladies and gentlemen,
boys and girls,
parents and grandparents.
I'm very happy to be here for
this jubilee and to see you all.
This is a great zoo with lots
of wonderful animals.
But all the children visiting
the animals are important, too.
Three cheers for the boys and girls!
Hip, hip – hurray!

Great, Mr Blümchen!
We love you, Benjamin!
Sensational!
Well done, Benjamin!
Goodbye!

This is a great zoo with lots of wonderful animals.
150
But all the children are important, too.
We love you, Benjamin!
Well done, Benjamin!

Wörter und Ausdrücke

Ein Brief aus England

dear – lieb, lieber, liebe, liebes
Mr (Mister) – Herr
please – bitte
to come – kommen
our – unser
zoo – Zoo
we – wir
to need – brauchen
you – du, dich
for – für
a – ein, eine
celebration – Feier
is – ist
to welcome – willkommen heißen
is welcome – ist willkommen
too – auch
are – sind
your – deine, Ihre, eure
ticket, tickets – Fahrkarte, Fahrkarten
best regards – mit freundlichen Grüßen
liontail – Löwenschwanz

Let's go to England together!

Let's go to England together! – Lass uns zusammen nach England fahren!
Wow! – Toll!
That's great! – Das ist toll / großartig!
English – Englisch, englisch
is easy and fun – ist leicht und macht Spaß
yes – ja
of course – natürlich, selbstverständlich
Good morning. – Guten Morgen.
everybody – jeder, jedermann; hier: alle miteinander
Hello! / Hi! – Hallo!
my name is – mein Name ist, ich heiße
Mrs – Frau
I – ich
I'm / I am – ich bin
I'm Mrs Kolumna. – Ich bin Frau Kolumna.
What? – Was?
you, too – du auch
How wonderful! – Wunderbar! Wie schön!
to go – gehen, fahren, reisen

together – zusammen
Let's go together. – Lasst uns zusammen gehen / fahren.
I mean – ich meine
Goodbye! – Auf Wiedersehen!
See you tomorrow! – Bis morgen!
mum and dad – Eltern (Mama und Papa)

Let's pack the suitcase!

Let's pack the suitcase! – Lass uns den Koffer packen!
suitcase – Koffer
to pack – packen
This is a suitcase. – Das ist ein Koffer.
we – wir
to need – brauchen, benötigen
What do we need? – Was brauchen wir?
I – ich
some trousers – eine Hose
a jacket – eine Jacke
right – richtig
a T-shirt – ein T-shirt
then – dann
my shoes – meine Schuhe
comb – Kamm
my toothbrusch – meine Zahnbürste
toothpaste – Zahnpasta
your things – deine Sachen / Dinge
Now let's pack your things. – Jetzt lass uns deine Sachen packen.
pyjamas – Schlafanzug
your pink pyjamas – dein rosa Schlafanzug
night cap – Schlafmütze, Nachtmütze
to put in – hineinstecken, hineinlegen; hier: einpacken
sugar lumps – Zuckerstückchen, Würfelzucker
a packet of sugar lumps – eine Packung Zuckerstückchen
What else do you need? – Was brauchst du sonst noch?
fluffy – flauschig, weich
towel – Handtuch
your nice, fluffy towel – dein schönes, kuschelweiches Handtuch
to forget – vergessen
don't forget – vergiss nicht
soap – Seife
alarm clock – Wecker
maybe – vielleicht
to know – wissen, kennen
you never know – du weißt nie, man kann nie wissen
well done – gut gemacht
to finish – beenden, fertigstellen, abschließen

we have finished / we've finished – wir sind fertig
railway station – Bahnhof
platform – Bahnsteig

Have a nice trip!

Have a nice trip! – Gute Fahrt!
trip – Reise, Fahrt, Ausflug
at last – endlich
late – spät, zu spät, verspätet
we're late – wir sind zu spät
to miss – verpassen, versäumen
train – Zug
We'll miss the train. – Wir werden den Zug verpassen.
to come – kommen
The train is coming. – Der Zug kommt.
to hurry up – sich beeilen
Hurry up! – Beeilt euch! / Beeil dich!
to have got – haben
luggage – Gepäck
We've got our luggage. – Wir haben unser Gepäck.
passport – Pass, Reisepass
everything – alles
time – Zeit
Have a nice time! – Eine schöne Zeit!
Thank you! – Danke!
All aboard! – Alles einsteigen!
quick – schnell, rasch
Let's get in quickly! – Lasst uns schnell einsteigen!
Bye-bye! – Wiedersehen! / Tschüss!

Travelling

travelling – Reisen
to travel – reisen
to make it – es schaffen
We've made it! – Geschafft! Wir haben es geschafft!
exciting – aufregend, spannend
here – hier
Here comes the train. – Hier kommt der Zug.
to run – fahren (laufen, rennen)
along – entlang
again – wieder
running along again – fährt wieder entlang
plane – Flugzeug
to fly – fliegen
car – Auto

fast – schnell
far – weit
going so fast and so far – fährt so schnell und so weit
truck, trucks – Lastauto, Lastautos
all – alle
row – Reihe
all in a row – alle in einer Reihe
ready – fertig, bereit
bus, buses – Bus, Busse
real – wirklich, tatsächlich, echt
really great – wirklich großartig, echt toll
bike, bikes – Fahrrad, Fahrräder
motorbike, motorbikes – Motorrad, Motorräder

On the ferryboat

on the ferryboat – auf der Fähre
ferryboat – Fähre, Fährschiff
big – groß
boat – Boot, Schiff
It's a really big boat. – Das ist wirklich ein großes Schiff.
with – mit
enormous – riesig, ungeheuer, gewaltig
anchor – Anker
with an enormous anchor – mit einem riesigen Anker
there are lifeboats – es gibt Rettungsboote
captain – Kapitän
Over there is the captain. – Dort ist der Kapitän.
sailor – Seemann, Matrose
on board – an Bord
Let's get on board! – Lasst uns an Bord gehen!
to hope – hoffen
I won't – ich werde nicht
to get – werden (oben: gehen)
seasick – seekrank
I won't get seasick. – Ich werde nicht seekrank.
to listen – hören, horchen, lauschen
horn – Horn, Hupe
Listen, that's the horn! – Hört, das ist das Schiffshorn!
We're ready to go. – Wir sind bereit zur Abfahrt.
lady, ladies – Dame, Damen
gentleman, gentlemen – Herr, Herren
Ladies and gentlemen! – Meine Damen und Herren!
old – alt
Old Mary – Alte Mary (Maria)
Welcome on board the "Old Mary"! – Willkommen an Bord der „Old Mary"!
crew – Mannschaft, Besatzung

his crew – seine Besatzung
to wish – wünschen
pleasant – angenehm, vergnüglich, erfreulich
journey – Reise, Fahrt, Tour
a pleasant journey to Dover – eine angenehme Fahrt nach Dover
Off we go! – Es geht los!
to look (at) – (an)schauen
Look at the captain! – Schau den Kapitän an!
to steer – steuern
He's / he is steering the boat. – Er steuert das Schiff.
seagull, seagulls – Möwe, Möwen
sky – Himmel
They're / They are flying in the sky. – Sie fliegen am Himmel.
fish, fish – Fisch, Fische
to swim – schwimmen
water – Wasser
Goodness! – Du meine Güte! Mein Gott!
shark, sharks – Hai, Haie
whale, whales – Wal, Wale
There are no sharks or whales. – Es gibt keine Haie und Wale.
seal, seals – Robbe, Robben / Seehund, Seehunde
dolphin, dolphins – Delphin, Delphine
but – aber
There are seals, but no dolphins. – Es gibt Robben, aber keine Delphine.
wave, waves – Welle, Wellen
wind – Wind
Listen to the waves and to the wind! – Höre den Wellen und dem Wind zu!
marvellous – wunderbar
Where is ...? – Wo ist ...?
to have to – müssen
to take – nehmen, hier: machen
picture – Bild, Foto
I have to take a picture! – Ich muss ein Foto machen! / Das muss ich fotografieren!

Welcome to London Zoo!

Welcome to London Zoo! – Willkommen im Londoner Zoo!
Hello, everybody! – Hallo, miteinander!
I'm – ich bin
from – von
nice – nett, schön
to meet – treffen, begegnen, kennen lernen
Nice to meet you. – Es ist nett, dich / Sie kennen zu lernen.
friend, friends – Freund / Freundin, Freunde
Are these your friends? – Sind das deine / Ihre Freunde?
reporter – Reporter, Reporterin
Look, these are my children. – Schaut, das sind meine Kinder.

child, children – Kind, Kinder
cup – Tasse
tea – Tee
a cup of tea – eine Tasse Tee
Let's have a cup of tea. – Lasst uns eine Tasse Tee trinken.
delicious – köstlich, lecker
That's a great idea! – Das ist eine großartige Idee!
marvellous – wunderbar

Benjamin's home in London

Benjamin's home in London – Benjamins Haus in London
home – Heim, Haus, Wohnung
house – Haus
This is your house. – Das ist dein Haus.
to like – mögen, gern haben
Do you like it? – Magst du es? / Gefällt es dir?
beautiful – schön
It's / It is beautiful. – Es ist schön.
to open – öffnen, aufmachen
door – Tür, Tor
Open the door! – Öffne die Tür! / Mach die Tür auf!
careful – vorsichtig
Be careful! – Sei vorsichtig!
enough – genug
Is the door big enough? – Ist die Tür groß genug?
to worry – sich beunruhigen, sich Sorgen machen
Don't worry! – Sei unbesorgt!
bed – Bett
table – Tisch
Here's a table. – Hier ist ein Tisch.
chair – Stuhl
some chairs – einige / ein paar Stühle
lamp – Lampe
There's a lamp. – Dort ist eine Lampe.
flower, flowers – Blume, Blumen
a bunch of flowers – ein Strauß Blumen, ein Blumenstrauß
to love – lieben
I love flowers. – Ich liebe Blumen.
also – auch
We also put a new green rug on the floor. –
Wir haben auch einen neuen, grünen Teppich auf den Boden gelegt.
to put – setzen, stellen, legen
new – neu
green – grün
rug – kleiner Teppich
floor – Boden, Fußboden

on the floor – auf den Boden
fire-place – Kamin
armchair – Sessel
to think – denken, meinen, glauben
time – Zeit
now – jetzt, nun, eben
It's time to go to bed now. – Es ist Zeit, jetzt ins Bett zu gehen.
must – müssen
very – sehr
tired – müde
You must be very tired. – Du musst / Ihr müsst sehr müde sein.
Good night! – Gute Nacht!
to sleep – schlafen
well – wohl, gut
Sleep well! – Schlaf gut!
tight – fest
Sleep tight! – Schlaf fest!
sweet – süß
dream, dreams – Traum, Träume
Have sweet dreams! – Träume süß!

Good morning, Benjamin, the sun is shining!

Good morning, Benjamin, ... – Guten Morgen, Benjamin, ...
... the sun is shining! – ... die Sonne scheint!
to get up – aufstehen
It's time to get up. – Es ist Zeit aufzustehen.
blue – blau
The sky is blue. – Der Himmel ist blau.
sun – Sonne
to shine – scheinen
The sun is shining ... – Die Sonne scheint ...
warm – warm
... and it's nice and warm. – ... und es ist schön warm.
weather – Wetter
today – heute
The weather is wonderful today. – Das Wetter ist herrlich heute.
cloudy – wolkig, bewölkt, trüb
It's not cloudy. – Es ist nicht bewölkt.
to rain – regnen
It's not raining. – Es regnet nicht.
windy – windig
cold – kalt
to snow – schneien
neither ... nor – weder ... noch
And it's neither cold nor snowing. – Und es ist weder kalt noch schneit es.
day – Tag

sunny – sonnig
a sunny day – ein sonniger Tag
to come – kommen
Come on! – Komm! / Los!
sleepy – schläfrig
head – Kopf
sleepyhead – Schlafmütze
ready – bereit, fertig
to get ready – sich fertig machen
Come on, sleepyhead, get up and get ready! –
Komm, du Schlafmütze, steh auf und mach dich fertig!

Getting ready

getting ready – sich fertig machen
to wake up – aufwachen
Benjamin is waking up. – Benjamin wacht auf.
to yawn – gähnen
to get out of bed – aus dem Bett aufstehen
to stretch – (sich) strecken / dehnen
Benjamin is stretching himself. – Benjamin streckt sich.
bathroom – Badezimmer
to sing – singen
to take off – ausziehen
shower – Dusche
to have a shower – (sich) duschen
to dry – (sich) abtrocknen
He's drying himself. – Er trocknet sich ab.
favourite – Lieblings-...
to get dressed – sich anziehen
Where is my red jacket? – Wo ist meine rote Jacke?
Here it is. – Hier ist sie.
Where are my blue trousers? – Wo ist meine blaue Hose?
Here they are, on the chair. – Hier ist sie, auf dem Stuhl.
cap – Mütze
in front of the mirror – vor dem Spiegel

Benjamin's body

body – Körper
trunk – Rüssel
nose – Nase
a trunk is an elephant's nose – ein Rüssel ist die Nase des Elefanten
long – lang
quite – ganz, recht, ziemlich
useful – nützlich
ear, ears – Ohr, Ohren

large – groß
two – zwei
two large ears – zwei große Ohren
right – richtig
eye, eyes – Auge, Augen
mouth – Mund
head – Kopf
All this is your head. – Das Ganze ist dein Kopf.
to have got – haben
hair – Haare
You haven't got any hair. – Du hast keine Haare.
Elephants don't have any hair. – Elefanten haben keine Haare.
elephant, elephants – Elefant, Elefanten
arm, arms – Arm, Arme
leg, legs – Bein, Beine
foot, feet – Fuß, Füße
round – rund
like – wie
hand, hands – Hand, Hände
tail – Schwanz
tummy – Bauch, Magen
Your tummy is the biggest. – Dein Bauch ist am größten.
fat – dick
empty – leer
to rumble – rumpeln; hier: knurren
Your tummy is rumbling. – Dein Magen knurrt.
to be hungry – hungrig sein
I'm very hungry. – Ich habe großen Hunger.
to be thirsty – Durst haben
all right – in Ordnung
breakfast – Frühstück
Let's have breakfast! – Lasst uns frühstücken!

Let's have breakfast!

milk – Milch
toast – Toast
butter – Butter
jam – Marmelade
honey – Honig
egg, eggs – Ei, Eier
scrambled eggs – Rühreier
Do you like scrambled eggs? – Magst du Rühreier?
no – nein
Sorry! – Es tut mir Leid!
No, I don't, sorry. – Nein, leider nicht.
but I do – aber ich

to love – lieben
yummy – lecker
cornflakes – Maisflocken
some – einige, etwas
strawberry, strawberries – Erdbeere, Erdbeeren
to eat – essen
What would you like to eat? – Was möchtest du gerne essen?
I'd like ... – Ich möchte gerne ... / Ich hätte gerne ...
please – bitte
me too – ich auch
lots of – viele, eine Menge
to know – wissen, kennen
They are very nice. – Sie sind sehr nett.

Lots of animals

lots of animals – viele Tiere
animal, animals – Tier, Tiere
to walk – gehen, spazieren
to walk round the zoo – im Zoo herumgehen
flamingo, flamingoes – Flamingo, Flamingos
to stand – stehen
pond – Teich, Weiher
They're standing in the pond. – Sie stehen im Teich.
bear, bears – Bär, Bären
lion, lions – Löwe, Löwen
to be called – genannt werden, heißen
cub – Junges, Jungtier
lion cub – Löwenjunges
cute – reizend, nett
giraffe, giraffes – Giraffe, Giraffen
tall – groß, lang, hoch
They're very tall ... – Sie sind sehr groß ...
with – mit
neck – Hals
.. with their long necks. – ... mit ihren langen Hälsen.
over there – dort drüben
bird, birds – Vogel, Vögel
owl – Eule
eagle – Adler
parrot – Papagei
a talking parrot – ein sprechender Papagei
How are you? – Wie geht es dir?
I'm fine! – Gut! / Es geht mir gut!
Thanks! – Danke!
crazy – verrückt
You're crazy! – Du bist verrückt! / Du spinnst!

hippo – Nilpferd, Hippopotamus
snake – Schlange
kangaroo – Känguru
camel – Kamel
panda – Panda
peacock – Pfau

The 10 monkeys

the 10 monkeys – die zehn Affen
monkey, monkeys – Affe, Affen
best – am meisten, am besten
I like the monkeys best. – Ich mag die Affen am liebsten/meisten.
funny – spaßig, komisch
this one – dieser (hier)
to climb – (hoch)klettern, (hinauf)steigen
tree – Baum
He is climbing up the tree. – Er klettert den Baum hinauf.
that one – dieser (dort)
to hang on – hängen an, sich klammern an
branch – Zweig, Ast
How many? – Wie viele?
to see – sehen
Can you see? – Kannst du / Könnt ihr sehen?
one – eins
two – zwei
three – drei
four – vier
to sit – sitzen
floor – Boden
to jump – springen
like – wie
frog – Frosch
to dance – tanzen
log – (gefällter) Baumstamm
to make – machen
that makes – das macht / ergibt
five – fünf
six – sechs
seven – sieben
eight – acht
nine – neun
ten – zehn

Balloons, colours and more

balloons, colours and more – Luftballons, Farben und mehr
balloon, balloons – Luftballon, Luftballons
colour, colours – Farbe, Farben
more – mehr
to stop – anhalten, aufhören
to blow – blasen
Stop blowing! – Hör auf zu blasen!
to burst – platzen
It'll / It will burst. – Er wird platzen.
It's / It has burst. – Er ist geplatzt.
What a pity! – We schade!
purple – lila
Never mind! – Macht nichts! / Mach dir nichts draus!
Here is another one. – Hier ist noch einer. / Hier ist ein anderer.
plenty of – viel / viele, eine Menge, reichlich
in all colours – in allen Farben
red – rot
blue – blau
green – grün
yellow – gelb
orange – orange
white – weiß
black – schwarz
brown – braun
grey – grau
there aren't any – es gibt keine
colourful – bunt
Chinese lantern – Lampion
paper chain – Girlande
How are you? – Wie geht es euch / dir?
to do – tun, machen
What are you doing? – Was macht ihr? / Was machst du?
I see. – Ich verstehe. / Ach so.
can – können
to help – helfen
Can I help you? – Kann ich euch/dir helfen?
first – zuerst
to keep ... – weiter ...
to smile – lächeln
Please, keep smiling! – Bitte (weiter)lächeln!
cheese – Käse
Sensational! – Sensationell!

The celebration

people – Leute
even – sogar
mayor – Bürgermeister
brass band – Blaskapelle
music – Musik
brass band music – Blasmusik
instrument, instruments – Instrumente
trumpets, trumpets – Trompete, Trompeten
drum, drums – Trommel, Trommeln
saxophone, saxophones – Saxophon, Saxophone
to play – spielen
choir – Chor
to sing – singen
song, songs – Lied, Lieder
must – müssen
happy – glücklich, froh
boy – Junge
girl – Mädchen
to want – wollen, wünschen
nervous – nervös, aufgeregt
I'm so nervous. – Ich bin so aufgeregt.
to manage – schaffen
You'll manage it! – Du wirst es schaffen!
sure – sicher, gewiss, bestimmt
I'm sure. – Ich bin sicher.
150th jubilee – 150. Jubiläum
year – Jahr
special – besondere, besonderer
guest – Gast
a very special guest – ein ganz besonderer Gast
to listen (to) – (zu)hören

Benjamin's speech

speech – Rede
luck – Glück
Good luck! – Viel Glück!
parents – Eltern
grandparents – Großeltern
to visit – besuchen, besichtigen
important – wichtig, bedeutend
are important – sind wichtig
cheers – Beifall(srufe), Jubel
Hurray! – Hurra!
Well done! – Gut gemacht!